simply wood

simply wood

22 elegantly rustic projects using
driftwood, logs, twigs and other found wood

Linda Suster

SEARCH PRESS

SEARCH PRESS

This edition published in Great Britain in 2020 by
Search Press Ltd
Wellwood
North Farm Road
Tunbridge Wells
Kent TN2 3DR
www.searchpress.com

Principal photography by Linda Suster

ISBN: 978-1-78221-816-6

This book was conceived, designed and produced by Toucan Books Ltd.
www.toucanbooks.co.uk

Suppliers
If you have difficulty in obtaining any of the materials and equipment mentioned in this book,
please visit the Search Press website for details of suppliers: www.searchpress.com

Printed in China

Contents

Introduction

Growing up on the Big Island of Hawaii, I began collecting shells, driftwood and other natural knick-knacks from an early age. Whenever wood washed up, I always liked to imagine the life it had led before reaching me. Moving to southern California in my early teens, I found driftwood on this new shore had a personality of its own. A wondrous array of different shapes, colours and textures introduced a whole new world to me! Once I had a family, I began an annual tradition of taking a week-long summer holiday from our home in sunny San Diego County to beautiful Lake Tahoe in northern California. Driving a different route each year allowed us to explore new riverbanks, lakefronts and coastlines.

This hobby of collecting unique twigs, branches, rocks and shells led to creating presents for family and friends. Their reactions inspired me to produce my projects on a larger scale! Since then, I have spent countless hours scouring the shores of lakes and oceans (where it is legal to take such items), or hunched over a piece, gluing in the tiniest detail. I have loved every second of creating items that have become the cherished possessions of others.

Nearly all of the wood featured in this book was hand-picked on my travels, and each piece holds a special memory of where I found it (see pages 108–113 for advice on collecting your own wood). Use pieces you have collected over the years to make the projects for yourself. Some techniques take more practice than others, and I know from experience how intimidating it can be to learn a new skill. Rest assured, the book is full of useful tips and easy-to-follow steps to keep you headed in the right direction. Just be sure to give yourself enough time to complete each of the steps. And, as with cooking, once the fire is hot, there is no time to waste, so be sure you have everything on hand before you begin.

Once you have tried a few things, do not be afraid to put your own spin on a project. My way is definitely not the only way, and if something feels more comfortable and seems like it is going to work, go for it!

Best of luck, and happy creating.

Linda

Twig

The Twig Vase on page 10 proves that even
the smallest twig can be transformed
into something useful for the home.
Larger twigs can be cut into lengths
and threaded together to become a
Christmas-tree-shaped work of art,
while a single sturdy twig supports
a tinkling row of glass chimes.

Twig Vase

With four components and minimal tools, you will build this woodland-themed vase in no time! The twigs hide a glass vase, which holds the water and flower stems.

MATERIALS

28–32 twigs, 14cm (5½in) long

Length of twine, 40.5cm (16in) long

Length of raffia ribbon, 101.5–122cm (40–48in) long

Jar, 14cm (5½ in) tall and 9cm (3½in) in diameter

TOOLS

Ruler

Drill with drill bit large enough to make a hole the diameter of the twine

Scissors

Twig Vase

1 Use a ruler to measure the centre of the length of each twig and drill a hole through the twigs at that point.

2 Decide on the order of the twigs, then thread the twine through the holes.

3 Arrange the twigs around the sides of the vase then tie the twine in a tight double knot (see page 120) to secure them. Cut the excess twine.

4 Wrap the raffia ribbon around the vase so that it hides the twine and tie in a double knot and then in a bow. Trim the ends of the ribbon to neaten them.

DESIGN IDEA

We decorated this vase with a rustic, raffia ribbon rather than the colourful red one on page 11. You can choose a bright or a neutral colour, or change the ribbon to suit your mood, the season or the flowers.

Twig Christmas Tree

Use this fun, festive tree to display your favourite ribbons and baubles. You will be able to use it year after year to celebrate the season and bring a splash of holiday cheer to your front door.

MATERIALS

Approximately 16 twigs of various sizes, 6.3cm (2½in) to 40.5cm (16in) long

Wooden star, 7.6cm (3in) wide

Two lengths of twine, 183cm (72in) long

Length of twine, 46cm (18in) long

Spools of yellow, blue and red ribbon, 0.5cm (¼in) wide

Spool of turquoise ribbon, 1cm (⅜in) wide

Christmas decorations such as baubles, bells, foliage and berry clusters

TOOLS

Band saw or strong pruning shears

Ruler

Scissors

Glue gun with glue sticks

Twig Christmas Tree

1 On a flat surface arrange the twigs in a triangle, with the shortest at the top and the longest at the base. If necessary, adjust the lengths using a band saw or strong pruning shears. Use the 183cm (72in) length of twine to tie the twigs together along one side, starting at the top and being sure to evenly space the pieces (see Tip, below). Repeat on the other side.

2 Tie the ends of the string at the base of the tree to secure them using a double knot (see page 120). Cut off the excess string.

3 Use the 46cm (18in) length of twine to tie the wooden star to the top of the tree using a double knot.

TIP

To tie the twigs together, wind one end of the twine around the top twig and tie a double knot (see page 120). Repeat for each twig until you reach the base. The twigs will look like a ladder.

4 Tie a bow around the star using the turquoise ribbon.

5 Tie lengths of the ribbons into bows and use a glue gun to attach them and the other decorations to the tree to create a balanced and festive effect.

Fish Wind Chime

Enjoy the sound of passing breezes tinkling through this nautical-themed wind chime. We have used glass fish to decorate it, but you can use any shape you like. Just make sure that the pieces of glass hang at an even length so that they knock against each other.

MATERIALS

28cm (11in) piece of driftwood, about 2.5cm (1in) thick

12 glass wind chime fish (available online)

12 lengths of twine, 20–25cm (8–10in) long

Length of twine, 30.5–35cm (12–14in) long

TOOLS

Ruler

Pencil

Drill with drill bit large enough to make a hole the diameter of the twine

Scissors

Fish Wind Chime

1 Using the ruler and pencil, mark twelve points about 2cm (¾in) apart along the length of the piece of driftwood. Drill a hole at each point.

2 Tie the twelve shorter lengths of twine to the glass fish using a double knot (see page 120), making sure they will hang evenly.

3 Thread the free end of each length of twine through one of the holes in the driftwood and secure with double knot (see page 120).

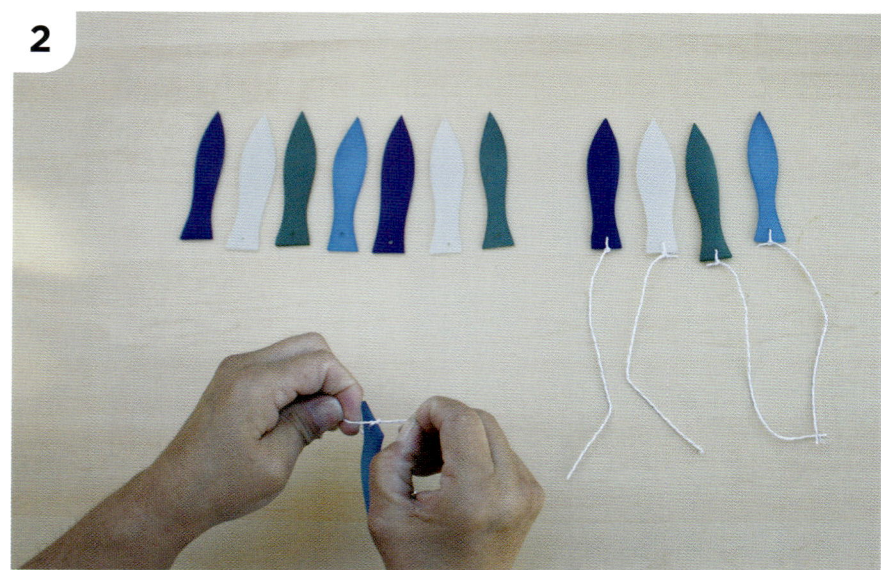

TIP

You can use as many, or as few, fish as you wish, just adjust the spaces between the holes so that they are an even distance apart. You can also adjust the lengths of the pieces of twine the fish hang from.

4 Drill a hole between the first and second knot on each end of the piece of driftwood.

5 Thread the longer length of twine through the top of each hole and knot at the bottom. Hang the wind chime from this piece of twine.

DESIGN IDEA

Instead of fish, look for other glass shapes online. Alternatively, string shells with holes drilled into them to create a wind chime fit for a mermaid. (For tips on drilling holes in shells, see page 53.)

Branch

Branches, whether thick and gnarled, straight or curving, provide many options for creativity. A single gnarled branch supports a trio of coat hooks while a row of sturdy branches set into a frame gives you a place to hang your hat. Entwined with twinkling lights, a cluster of branches becomes a rustic chandelier.

Trio of Coat Hooks

Look for a branch with an intriguing shape that is large and sturdy enough to hold three metal coat hooks. The finished piece will add rustic charm to a hallway.

MATERIALS

Branch (size will depend on preference and availability)

Sawtooth hanger

Three coat hooks with screws

TOOLS

Hand planer, if required

Drill

Pencil

Trio of Coat Hooks

1 If the back of the branch needs to be flattened to enable it to sit flush against the wall, use a hand planer to smooth the surface.

2 Attach the hanger to the back of the branch by following the package instructions.

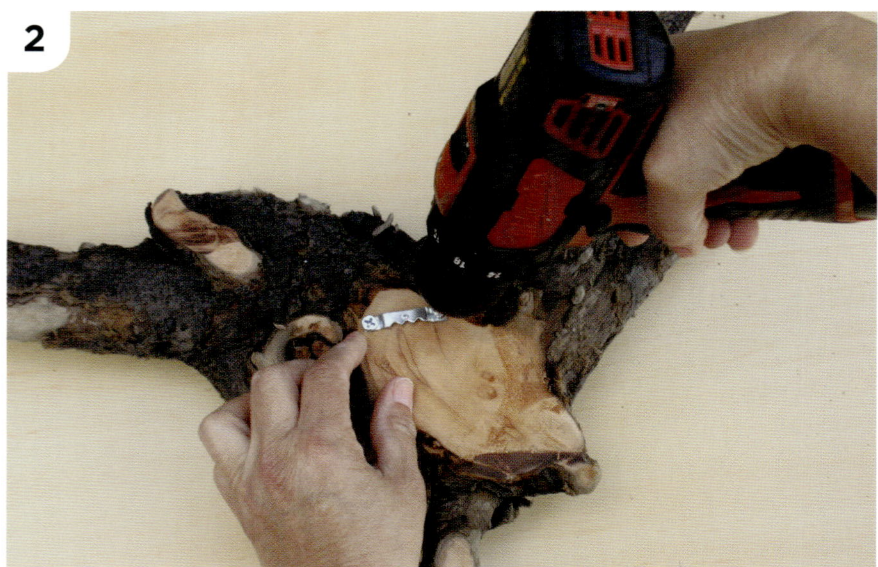

TIP

When using a planer, always remember to go 'with the grain', as you would when sanding. For more tips on planing, see page 114.

3 On the front of the branch, use a pencil to mark the desired locations of the coat hooks. Make a pencil mark for the position of each screw required to hold the hooks in place.

4 Drill pilot holes at the marked locations.

5 Use the screws provided to secure the hooks to the branch. Attach the coat rack to the wall using the hanger.

Branch Chandelier

Bring a little bit of the forest into your home and add a touch of whimsy to any dinner party with this simple chandelier. The branches that make up this chandelier hang from a metal ring and are decorated with a string of sparkly, battery-operated lights.

MATERIALS

Four or five branches, 76–91.5cm (30–36in) long

Battery-operated LED string lights, with batteries

Metal ring, 5cm (2in) diameter

1.8–2.4m (6–8ft) of rustic-looking rope

Two lengths of small gauge, bendable wire, 35–40.5cm (14–16in) and 91.5cm (36in) long

TOOLS

Brush

Pruning shears

Scissors

Wire-cutting pliers

Branch Chandelier

1 Use the brush to clean any debris or loose pieces from the branches. Arrange the branches so that they fit together at the bases and flare out at the tips.

2 Use a pair of pruning shears to remove any excess twigs from the bottom 15cm (6in) of the branches so that they will fit together closely at the base.

3 Use the shorter length of wire to secure the battery pack for the lights to the base of one of the branches by wrapping it around and through the pack. Make sure that the on/off switch on the pack remains accessible.

4 Cluster the other branches around the branch with the battery pack attached so that the ends flare out. Tie the branches together at the base using the longer length of wire, being careful to keep the battery pack on the outside of the cluster.

5 Tie the length of rope around the metal ring and secure with a double knot (see page 120). Insert one branch into the ring.

6 Wedge the rope knot through the centre of the cluster of branches and tighten it. Then wrap the rope around the cluster to hide the battery pack, making sure you can still access the on/off switch.

7 Tie a double knot at the top of the chandelier close to the ring to secure everything in place.

8 Arrange the lights on the chandelier so that the lights are distributed throughout the branches.

TIP

You may need a second pair of hands to help you to stabilize the chandelier while you insert the branch and rope into the ring in step 5.

TIP

Use the metal ring to hang the chandelier from a ceiling hook or a sturdy light fixture that includes a hook.

Rustic Coat Rack

Your house guests are sure to love this rustic coat rack, a great addition to any hallway! Use branches that are at least 2.5cm (1in) in diameter so that they are sturdy enough to hold coats and bags, as well as hats and the dog's lead.

MATERIALS

Seven sturdy twigs, at least 30.5cm (12in) long

Two pieces of reclaimed wood, 30.5 x 7.6cm (12 x 3in)

Two pieces of reclaimed wood, 76.2 x 7.6cm (30 x 3in)

22 2cm (¾in)
3.5mm (⅛in) diameter screws

Two sawtooth hangers with screws

TOOLS

Heavy-duty pruning shears

Mitre saw

Drill with drill and screwdriver bits

Rustic Coat Rack

1 Use the heavy-duty pruning shears to trim the twigs so they are all 30.5cm (12in) long. Arrange them on a flat surface in the desired order.

2 On a flat surface, arrange the pieces of reclaimed wood to create a rectangular frame that will fit the twigs. Secure the pieces of wood together at the corners, using two screws at each corner. There is no need to drill pilot holes.

TIP
Use branches that are from the same type of tree and at least 2.5cm (1in) thick with lots of smaller branches coming off them to make the 'rack' spots. One way to achieve this is to find a long branch and cut it into 30.5cm (12in) pieces.

3 Arrange the twigs inside the frame so that they are at the front edge and spaced evenly. Secure the twigs to the frame using a screw at each end of each twig. There is no need to drill pilot holes.

4 Decide on the position of the sawtooth hangers – as they will bear the weight of the coat rack they should be about 2.5–3.8cm (1–1½in) in from each edge. Drill pilot holes into the back of the frame, then secure the hangers with screws.

Driftwood

Smoothed by the sea and bleached by the sun, driftwood is my favourite material. From the decorative, a simple sailing boat or a hanging sculpture, to the elegant, a mirror set in a corolla of twigs or a frame adorned with shells, to the practical, a rustic bottle opener or a tea light candleholder – there is a project to showcase any item of driftwood you bring home from the shore.

Sunburst Wall Mirror

This beautiful statement piece with its sunburst design makes an eye-catching centrepiece for any wall. You can use driftwood for this project, but as you need 100 pieces, you may find it easier to source suitable twigs.

MATERIALS

30.5cm (12in) particle board floral craft ring

Brown paint, or the colour of your choice

About 100 thick, 12.5–15cm (5–6in) long twigs

25.4cm (10in) diameter mirror

Sawtooth hanger with accompanying screws

TOOLS

Paintbrush

Strong multipurpose craft glue

Drill with bit for sawtooth hanger

DESIGN IDEA

To make the piece even more dramatic, add a ring of driftwood pieces around the mirror. Lay the finished piece face up on a work surface and arrange the pieces to make a circular frame. Glue them using the technique for the Shabby Chic Candleholder (see page 54).

Sunburst Wall Mirror

1 Paint the particle board ring and leave to dry.

2 Arrange a base layer of pieces of wood around the ring, aligning one end of each piece of wood with the inside edge of the frame. When you are happy with their positions, secure the pieces of wood with glue. Leave to dry.

TIP

Instead of using a floral craft ring as the base for this mirror, you could use a rectangular, heart-shaped or other frame.

3 Glue a second layer of wood on top of the base layer to add depth and texture. Position the pieces of wood between the pieces on the first layer. Leave to dry. Arrange a ring of twigs around the central hole in the frame. Leave to dry.

4 Carefully lay the twig frame face down on a clean work surface. Position the mirror so that the glass is face down and centred in the middle of the frame. Glue in place and leave to dry.

5 Decide where you want the top of the frame to be and add the sawtooth hanger at the top by attaching it to the particle board ring. To do this, drill two shallow pilot holes, then insert the screws. Hang the mirror on the wall.

DESIGN IDEA

The frame can be used without a mirror to make a stunning wall hanging.

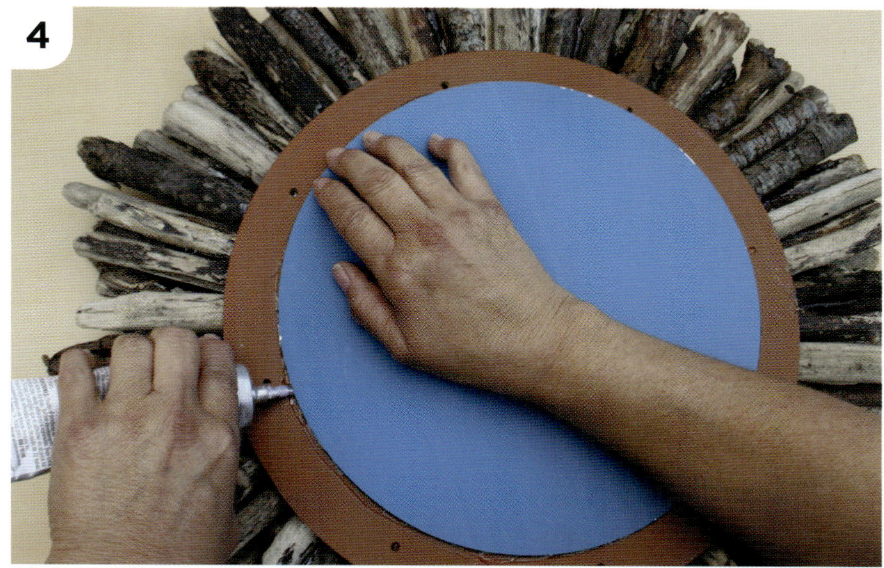

Miniature Sailing Boat

Keep your memories of life at the beach – or on the water – alive by displaying this cute sailing boat in your home. Even if you live far from the shore, it will be a daily reminder of sunny days with the wind in your hair and maybe the sand between your toes.

MATERIALS

Flat piece of driftwood, 18–23cm (7–9in) long and 10–12.5cm (4–5in) wide

Piece of 1cm (⅜in) wooden dowel, 30.5cm (12in) long

Piece of patterned fabric, 21.6 x 28cm (8½ x 11in)

Length of ribbon, approximately 10cm (4in) long

Two bronze furniture tacks, or similar wood screws with a head or hook to secure twine around

Length of twine, approximately 122cm (48in) long

TOOLS

Pen

Ruler

Scissors

Piece of scrap wood or corkboard to use as a drilling base

Drill with a drill bit the same size as the dowel you are using

Large-eyed needle

Damp kitchen towel or cotton bud

Fabric glue

Wood glue

Miniature Sailing Boat

1 Fold the fabric in half on the diagonal to make a triangle. Use a pen and ruler to mark a straight line along the diagonal fold. Cut the fabric in half along the marked line.

2 Place the pieces of fabric on a work surface with the wrong sides towards you and the long vertical edges touching, so that they form a triangular sail. Place the length of dowel along the join in the fabrics to create the mast, leaving a small space at the top and 6.3cm (2½in) of the dowel exposed at the base. Apply glue to the central part of the dowel, leaving the top and bottom bare. Fold both pieces of fabric over the dowel and press to seal. Leave to dry.

3 Fold the length of twine in half to find the centre and position the top of the dowel in the fold. Wrap the twine around the top of the dowel at the tip of the fabric sail, and tie a double knot (see page 120) to secure it.

4 Now wrap both ends of the twine twice around the dowel, wrapping one either side of the knot. Leave enough twine at each end to secure at the back of the dowel using a double knot.

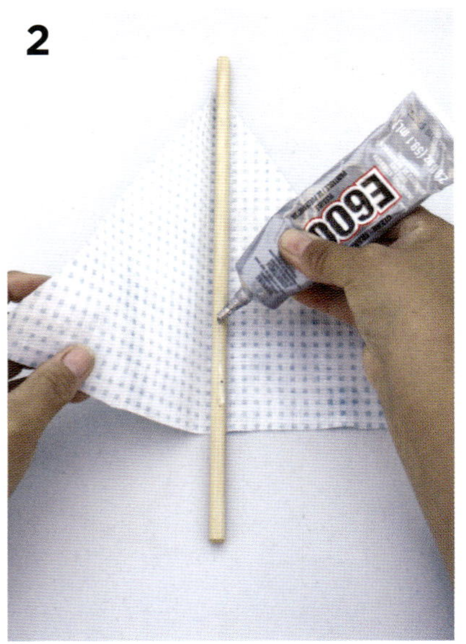

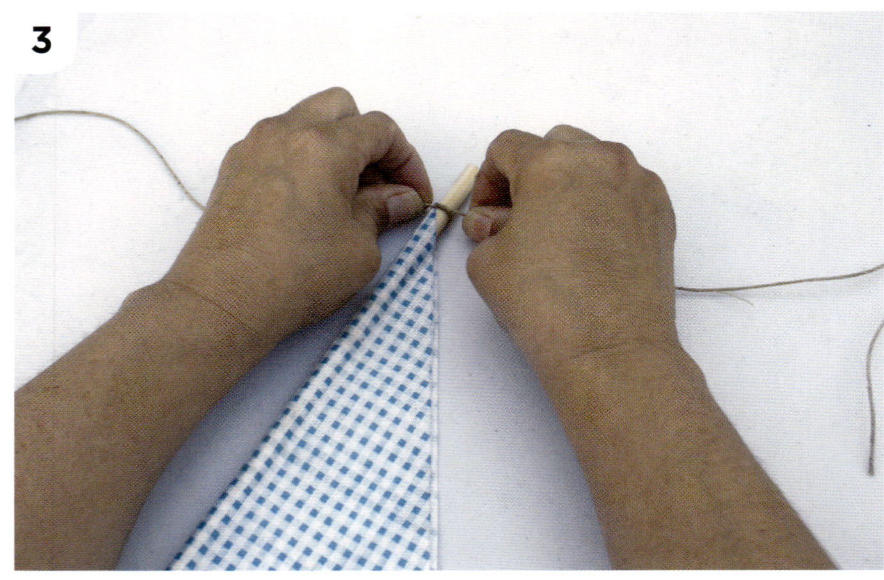

5 Thread one end of the twine through a large-eyed needle and stitch through the open edge side of the sail, creating six evenly spaced running stitches. Leave the other piece of twine free at the top of the sail.

6 Drill a shallow hole 1.3–2cm (½–¾in) deep and the diameter of the dowel, 5–7.6cm (2–3in) from one end of the piece of driftwood. Place a generous drop of wood glue into the drilled hole, insert the dowel, wipe away the excess glue using a damp cloth or cotton bud, and leave to dry completely.

7 Insert a furniture tack into the centre of each end of the driftwood base so that it is secure but still protrudes from the wood.

8 Wrap the free end of one of the lengths of twine around one of the tacks as many times as needed to keep it taut. Add a dab of fabric glue to secure. Repeat with the end of the other length of twine and the second tack.

9 Fold the length of ribbon in half and cut a V-shape into the cut ends. Wrap it around the top of the dowel, above the sail, and glue it in place. Let dry completely.

Seaside Mirror

Whimsical and beachy, this mirror will bring
a touch of the seashore into your home.

MATERIALS

20.3 x 25.4cm (8 x 10in)
rectangular mirror

Two 15–20cm (6–8in) pieces of
driftwood

Two 25.4–30.5cm (10–12in) pieces
of driftwood

Two 35–40.5cm (14–16in) pieces
of driftwood

Eight or ten shells

TOOLS

Strong multipurpose craft glue

Ruler

Seaside Mirror

1 On a work surface, place the two 35–40.5cm (14–16in) pieces of driftwood parallel to each other 19cm (7½in) apart with the right sides facing up.

2 Arrange the two 25.4–30.5cm (10–12in) pieces of driftwood at the ends of the longer pieces to create a frame. Secure with glue.

3 Arrange the two 15–20cm (6–8in) pieces of driftwood on the longer, vertical sections of the frame as desired. Secure with glue.

4 Arrange the shells on the frame as desired and glue in place. Let the glue dry before proceeding to the next step.

5 Gently turn the frame over and lay it face down on the work surface. Add a thin line of glue to each vertical interior edge of the wood (only the parts that will touch the mirror) and lay the mirror face down onto the wood and so that it is centred. Press into place to ensure the glue is in contact with all the surfaces. Leave to dry completely before turning over and using.

DESIGN IDEA

Instead of inserting a mirror you can use the frame to hold a favourite photograph. Simply attach a magnetic clip frame to the back using a strong multipurpose craft glue. Then you can change the photograph if you wish.

Driftwood Sculpture

For this project, you can use a selection of treasured items – driftwood, a shell or even a length of rope, if you are lucky! If not you can purchase some additions. Either way, you are sure to make a sculpture that is perfect, no matter where you hang it!

MATERIALS

40 to 60 pieces of driftwood, 10–12.5cm (4–5in) long

Length of rope, 91.5–122cm (36–48in) long

One to three beads or one shell, depending on how you want to hang and finish the sculpture

TOOLS

Pencil

Piece of scrap wood or corkboard to use as a drilling base

Drill with drill bit the same size as the rope you are using

Brush

Scissors

Strong multipurpose craft glue

Driftwood Sculpture

1 Arrange all the pieces of wood in a row and decide on their order for the sculpture. Measure each one and mark the central point with a pencil.

2 Using the scrap wood or corkboard as a base to protect your work surface, drill a hole through each piece of wood and remove any debris with a brush.

TIP

You can measure the central point of each piece of wood – or simply estimate it. If you choose not to measure the wood, the finished sculpture will look more organic.

3 Prepare the rope. You can simply make a loop to hang the sculpture from (as here), or you can knot it around a bead or through a hole drilled in a shell (see Tip, below) using a double knot (see page 120).

4 String the rope through the pieces of wood, keeping them in the desired order – you can choose to make it as taut or loose as you would like.

5 Once all the pieces are on the rope together, make sure the sculpture is at the desired tautness, then tie off the bottom in a double knot. Add some dabs of glue in the folds of the knot to secure it.

TIP

If you are using shells as well as twigs, be careful as you drill into them. Some shells, such as sand dollars and starfish, are delicate and will not require very much pressure to drill, while others, such as large clams, are extremely strong and thick and will take patience to break through!

Shabby Chic Candleholder

Instantly add rustic charm to any table setting with this tea light candle decoration. Small pieces of driftwood are arranged so that they hold a glass candleholder. We finished ours with a votive candle, but you can choose any candle you have on hand that fits your glass.

MATERIALS

10 to 15 piece of driftwood of varying sizes ranging from 7.6cm (3in) to 15cm (6in) long

Small glass votive candleholder

Small votive candle

TOOLS

Pencil

Cotton bud and damp paper towel (optional)

Strong multipurpose craft glue

Shabby Chic Candleholder

1 Arrange the pieces of wood in a tapered tower with the largest pieces criss-crossing each other to form the base, and the smaller, more curved pieces at the top to hold the glass candleholder. Make sure the hole in the centre of the top layer is large enough to fit the candleholder but small enough to hold it firmly.

2 When you are happy with the arrangement of the pieces, make a pencil mark at the point of best contact between each one.

SAFETY

Before gluing the last layer of the wood, make sure the top of the glass candleholder will sit above the wood so there is no danger of the wood catching fire.

3 Take apart the tower, making a note of where the pieces go. Starting with the first layer, carefully add a dab of glue on each pencil mark. Join the pieces together and set aside for 20 to 30 minutes, or until the glue has dried, before assembling the next layer.

4 Repeat step 3 for each layer of wood.

5 The last layer needs to be tight enough to hold the glass candleholder in place as well as support the weight of both the glass candleholder and the candle. You may want to size it a little on the snug side and then wedge the candleholder in place when the glue is completely dry. Join the final pieces together and, when the glue has dried, insert the candleholder and candle.

TIP

If you are nervous about applying the glue to the pieces of wood directly from the tube, use a cotton bud to apply it and have a damp paper towel handy to wipe off any excess.

Woodsy Opener

This bottle opener is sure to be a conversation piece at any party – just try not to brag too much about your crafting skills! You can mount the bottle opener to any secure, vertical surface where it will always be on hand.

MATERIALS

43–45.7cm (17–18in) piece of driftwood

Bottle opener

Two 2.5cm (1in) screws for the bottle opener

Two 7.6cm (3in) anchor screws to secure the bottle opener to the wall

Four lengths of twine 15cm (6in) long (or two pieces each long enough to wrap around your piece of driftwood twice)

TOOLS

Table saw

Pencil

Drill

Piece of scrap wood or corkboard to use as a drilling base

Drill bit the same size as the 2.5cm (1in) screws

Drill bit slightly larger than the size of the 7.6cm (3in) screws

Screwdriver with same head as screws

Scissors

Wood glue

Woodsy Opener

1 Decide which side of the piece of driftwood will be the front. Use a table saw to shave the back of the piece of driftwood so it will rest flat against the wall.

2 Place the bottle opener in the desired position on the front of the driftwood and use a pencil to mark the position of each short screw. Drill shallow pilot holes (less than 2.5cm/1in deep) into the wood. Secure the bottle opener to the driftwood using the 2.5cm (1in) screws.

3 Measure the point 6.3cm (2½in) from each end (the top and bottom) of the driftwood and drill a pilot hole using a drill bit slightly larger than the 7.6cm (3in) screws.

TIP

The holes drilled in the top and bottom of the driftwood will be used to secure the bottle opener to the wall using the long screws. Be sure the screws easily pass through the wood so that you can secure the bottle opener to the wall.

4 To mark the position of the twine accents, measure the points 5cm (2in) above and below the bottle opener and make a small pencil mark. Wrap the twine around the driftwood twice at this point and secure using wood glue. Let dry completely.

5 Decide the place on the wall where you want the bottle opener to hang. Holding the bottle opener in place, drill through the pilot holes in the driftwood and into the wall at the top of the opener, then insert one of the long screws and tighten. Repeat at the bottom of the opener.

TIP

The bottle opener needs to be secure since you will be leveraging bottle tops against it to open them. Rather than drilling pilot holes into the wall first, it is best to screw it directly into the wall (or tree!).

Log

Sturdy and rustic, logs bring the spirit of the woods into your home. From the simple, a table made from a slice of wood mounted on metal legs, to complex assemblages of logs, boards and branches, there is a project to suit every skill level. An elegant lamp base and a colourfully upcycled planter round off the offerings in this chapter.

Neat Two-seater

You will feel like a true woodsman building this rustic hall bench made completely from found logs and sturdy branches.

MATERIALS

Four pieces of reclaimed wood for the cross braces, 30.5cm (12in) long x 2.5cm (1in) wide

Four pieces of reclaimed wood for the legs, 46cm (18in) tall x 6.3–9cm (2½–3½in) wide

Four pieces of reclaimed wood for the length supports, 91.5cm (36in) long x 2.5cm (1in) wide

20–24 slats for the bench, 46cm (18in) long and of varying widths and textures

16 6.3cm (2½in) screws

40–48 screws, 4mm (³/₁₆in) in diameter and 4cm (1⅝in) long (two for each slat)

TOOLS

Table saw

Mitre saw

Drill with drill bit the same size as the screws, 2.5cm (1in) flare bit and screwdriver bit

Measuring tape

Pencil

Neat Two-seater

1 Reduce the size of the ends of the wood selected for the cross braces by making a series of quick cuts so that they will fit the 2.5cm (1in) holes you will make with the flare bit.

2 Use the flare bit to make connecting holes at the end of each leg. Rotating the leg so that the holes are at a 90-degree angle, drill another hole 20.3cm (8in) below the first set of holes, to act as a second set of support holes. Repeat on all four legs.

3 Drill a pilot hole in each flare hole. (In each set, one pilot hole should angle downwards and the other upwards so that the screws do not collide.)

TIP
When working on the slats, sand down any rough edges on the wood and decide whether you want to countersink the screws so they sit flush with the surface of the bench (see page 118).

4 On one side of the
bench, fit the cross brace
pieces into the hole and
then insert the 6.3cm
(2½in) screws. Repeat for
the other side. Prop both
sides up and insert the
length supports. Insert
the screws. Repeat on the
other side.

5 Lay the slat pieces across
the top of the completed
bench base. Drill a pilot
hole in each end where
the slat lies over the
length supports. Repeat
for each slat.

6 Insert a 4cm (1⅝in) screw
through each pilot hole
to secure a slat to the
length support. Repeat
for each slat.

Birch Log Bookshelf

This elegant shelving unit will add natural appeal to any wall in your home. Use it to display books, cherished items and photos.

MATERIALS

Five shelves, cut to varying lengths 91.5–122cm (36–48in) and to widths of 12.5–2Ccm (5–8in); maple, poplar and birch are all good choices

Eight to ten birch lcgs, cut in pairs of varying lengths between 20–30.5cm (8–12in) (some of the logs will be decorative and will not need a partner)

Four screw-on furniture legs in your desired colour/texture (the type suitable for a sofa or chair)

16–20 screws, 4mm ($\frac{3}{16}$in) in diameter and 4cm ($1\frac{5}{8}$in) long (two for each log you intend to use)

400 grit sandpaper

Wood plugs (optional)

Two L-shaped brackets

TOOLS

Hand sander

Mitre saw

Measuring tape or ruler

Pencil

Drill with drill bits

Scrap wood

Rubber mallet

Strong multipurpose craft glue

Birch Log Bookshelf

1 Sand the top of each shelf to ensure a smooth surface. Select the piece you would like to be the top of the bookshelf and set aside.

2 Measure the logs to check the lengths. You will need a pair of support logs for each shelf. The number of decorative logs of varying lengths you require will depend on your preference. In the example shown here, there are eight support logs and two decorative logs.

3 Cut the logs to the desired measurement.

4 Work out the position of the logs. It does not necessarily matter how far in on each side the logs go, as long as they are centred on the width of the shelf. The example shown is 91.5cm (36in) long and 14cm (5½in) wide. For the shelf shown here, the log is centred 7cm (2¾in) on the width and 22.8cm (9in) from the long edge. Use a pencil to mark the position of the screws for the logs.

5 Lay a piece of scrap wood down on the work surface and place the shelf on top of it. Drill a pilot hole through the shelf on the two points marked in step 4.

6 Using a drill bit that is the same size as the head of the screw, drill a pilot hole the depth of the wood plug on both sides of the shelf.

7 Drill a shallow pilot hole into the two logs being used for this shelf.

Birch Log Bookshelf

Before proceeding, decide which method of masking the screws you want to use. Option one is to use wood plugs to hide the screw heads. If you do not want to buy wood plugs, the other option is to save some of the sawdust from the project, add a dab of glue on top of each screw and sprinkle the sawdust into the hole. With both options, the important thing to remember is that you will have to countersink the screws (see Techniques, page 118).

8 Start to insert the screws through the pilot holes in the shelf by hand.

9 Holding the log against the screw, drill the screw through both the log and shelf to secure. Repeat for the other pilot hole.

10 Be sure to countersink the screws so they are below the surface of the shelf to leave room for the wood plug.

11 Depending on which option for masking the screws you have chosen (see box above), cover the screws. Wood plugs are shown here. Add a dab of glue to each screw head and place the wood plug into the hole.

12 Use a rubber mallet to gently tap the wood plug until it is flush with the shelf.

13 Next, attach the second shelf. Repeat steps 4 and 5 to measure where you want the logs to go and drill the pilot holes. Attach the shelf following the instructions in steps 6–12. Repeat the process until the desired number of shelves is complete.

14 When you have the desired number of shelves, add the furniture legs. There will be two legs on each side. Make sure they are evenly spaced. Using a drill bit slightly thinner than the leg screw, drill a pilot hole around the same length as the screw.

15 Insert the furniture legs. Repeat the process on the other side.

SAFETY

For extra security, be sure to secure the bookshelf to the wall with a couple of small L-shaped brackets.

Chunky Table

Add a touch of mid-century glamour to your yard or living room by creating this simple end table. Look for a section of log with an attractive shape and interesting markings for a piece of furniture that will be as useful as it is eye-catching.

MATERIALS

Cut log for the tabletop; the one shown measures 35 x 28cm (14 x 11in) and is 8.2cm (3¼in) thick

Three to four metal hairpin table legs, 40.5cm (16in) tall and with clip-on floor protectors (available online)

16 screws, 4mm (³⁄₁₆in) in diameter and 3.1cm (1¼in) long

TOOLS

Hand sander

Drill

1 Decide which side of the log will be the top of the table and use a hand sander to sand it smooth.

2 Place the sanded side of the tabletop face down on a clean work surface. Arrange the legs in the desired configuration and secure with the screws. Clip on the floor protectors.

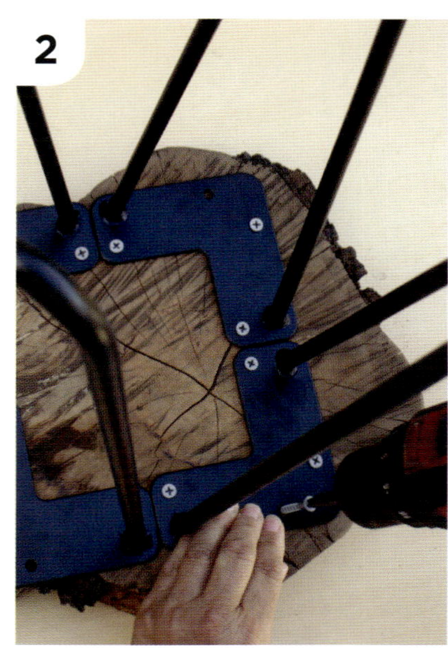

Vibrant Vertical Planter

Whether in your garden or among potted plants on your balcony, this playfully rustic planter is sure to brighten anyone's day! Choose cans large enough to hold your favourite flowering plants, or perhaps you prefer cascades of tomatoes, herbs or strawberries.

MATERIALS

Three cans

Acrylic, waterproof paint in colours of your choice

Four pieces of scrap pallet wood each 20–25cm (8–10in) long

Eight screws – we used 4cm (1⅝in) Phillips-head screws, but any 5cm (2in) grey screw will work well

Log, 91.5–122cm (36–48in) long and 10cm (4in) in diameter

TOOLS

Paintbrushes or sponges

Table saw, or a similar setup

Drill with Phillips-head drill bit and drill bit for pilot holes ($\frac{1}{32}$ size works well for these screws)

Vibrant Vertical Planter

1 Paint your cans and let them dry (see Tip, below).

2 While the painted cans are drying, use the scrap pallet wood to make a base. Cut all four pieces the same length (about 20–25cm/8–10in) and create a pinwheel-shaped base with a central opening large enough to hold the log securely. Size it so that it is snug enough to hold the log on its own, but not so tight that you will not be able to tighten it if needed.

3 Holding two of the base pieces together, drill a pilot hole where the pieces of wood have the strongest connection (see page 118). Then, drill the screws in to secure the base pieces together. Repeat until all pieces are secured.

4 Insert the log into the completed base. Holding it in place, drill pilot holes on each side of the base, then insert the screws into each hole and tighten them to secure it.

5 When your log has been secured into the base on all sides, it is time to add the cans. Decide which side you want to be the front of the first can, and drill a pilot hole through the metal on the opposite side, which will be the back. Decide where you will position the can on the log and attach it with a screw. You can create another pilot hole or just drill straight into the wood. Repeat with the remaining cans.

Log-stack Lamp

Brighten the corner of a room and get that expensive handcrafted look at a fraction of the cost (and you will have the satisfaction of making it with your own hands)! This lamp base is formed from discs of wood stacked on top of each other.

MATERIALS

Log, 7.6–10cm (3–4in) in diameter and 35.5cm (14in) long

Lamp kit

Lamp harp or UNO lampshade adapter

Wood glue

Lampshade

TOOLS

Mitre saw

Ruler

Pencil

Drill with drill bit the same size as the lamp cord

Piece of scrap wood or corkboard to use as a drilling base

Needle-nosed pliers

Log-stack Lamp

1 Mark 2.5cm (1in) spaces along the log. Use the mitre saw to cut the log into fourteen pieces 2.5cm (1in) thick.

2 Find the centre of the pieces of wood by measuring them vertically and horizontally and marking the point where the lines intersect. Using a piece of scrap wood or corkboard as a drilling base, drill a hole through the centre of each one.

3 Select the piece of wood that will form the base of the lamp and drill a second hole horizontally through the centre of one side; this hole should connect with the existing central hole but should not extend beyond the hole. It will form a channel for the cord.

4 Thread the lamp cord through the base, starting with the horizontal hole. Then thread it through the remaining pieces of wood. If necessary, use a pencil to push it into the holes and needle-nosed pliers to pull it through.

5 Following the package instructions, fit the lamp kit to the top of the pieces of wood. Position the base of the lamp socket in the drilled hole. Secure the wiring using an underwriter's knot (see page 121). Connect the wiring into the main socket by loosening the screw, hooking the end of the wire around the terminal and tightening the screw. Repeat this on the other terminal.

6 Push the socket together so that the wiring is on the inside. Secure with a screw.

7 Secure the socket to the base following the package instructions.

8 Working downwards from the top of the lamp, use wood glue to secure each piece of wood to the next until you reach the base. Leave to dry completely.

9 Add the lamp harp or shade adapter to hold the shade and the bulb.

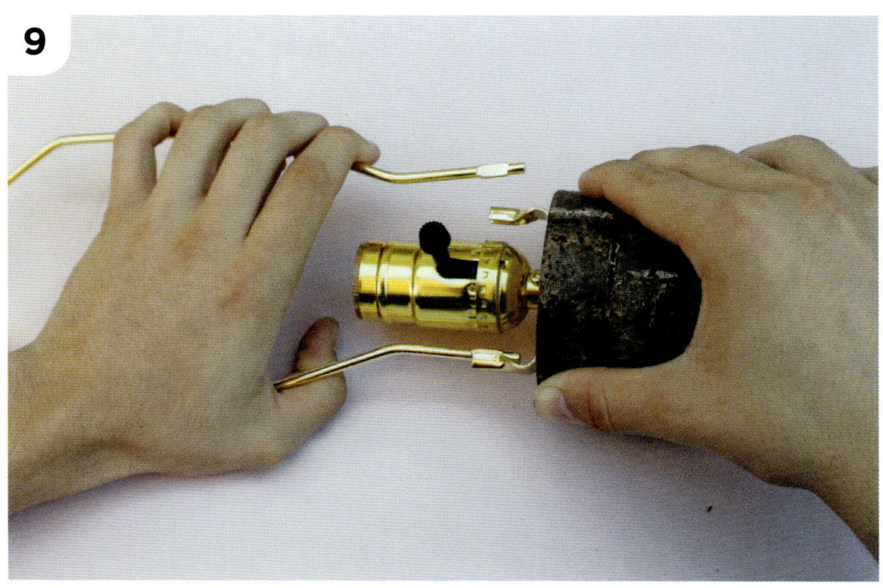

Board

Whether you have a short piece of board or a whole pallet, this chapter shows you how to make something beautiful out of it. Using boards you can make a sign, build a shelf or a tray for the bath, put together a planter or create a clock. Let the wood speak for itself or embellish your creations with stencils to provide the perfect finishing touch.

Beach This Way!

Whether you want to point the way to the beach, your garden or your kitchen, this sign will show guests the way.

MATERIALS

Piece of board about 10 x 20cm (4 x 8in)

Two small nails or tacks

Length of twine, 35–40.5cm (14–16in)

Glue (optional)

White paint

TOOLS

Hammer

Foam paintbrush

Stencil saying 'beach' with an arrow, sized about 5.7 x 15cm (2¼ x 6in) (see page 122)

Repositionable spray adhesive or low-tack masking tape

TIP
You can spell out any word or message you like. Just remember to choose a piece of board long enough to hold all the letters you need.

beach

Beach This Way!

1 Holding the piece of board horizontally, attach a nail at each side edge, positioning them 1.3cm (½in) down from the top edge.

2 Secure the ends of the twine around each nail using a simple knot. You can add a dab of glue to secure the knots if you wish.

3 Place your stencil in the desired position on the piece of wood and secure in place using repositionable spray adhesive or low-tack masking tape.

4 Lightly dab paint onto the stencil to fill in the letters, being careful not to put too much paint under the edges of the letters. Carefully remove the stencil and leave to dry.

STENCILLING METHODS

Stencilling is easy when you know how. You can either use a ready-made template (see pages 122–125) or create your own stencil. Once you have mastered the art of stencilling, you can add a touch of whimsy and fun to your wood projects.

MAKING A CUSTOM STENCIL

To create a bespoke stencil, photocopy or trace the letters you need onto a sheet of paper and cut them out. The method below guarantees that your letters will be straight and evenly spaced.

- Use a ruler and pen or pencil to draw a straight line onto a piece of card or sheet of plastic. Copy or trace the letters onto the card or plastic using the line as a guide to ensure that they are straight.

- When you are happy with the placement of the letters, use a sharp pair of scissors to cut out each one, making sure the edges are neat. You will apply the paint through the holes you have created.

- Alternatively, type your letters into a word processing program and print them out, scaling them up or down so that they fit your piece of wood. Copy or trace the letters and then cut them out as before.

- Once your stencil is ready, position it over your piece of wood and secure in place with repositionable spray glue or low-tack masking tape.

- Dip the tip of your paintbrush into the paint and dab off the excess onto a piece of scrap paper – it is better to build up several thin layers of paint until you have the coverage you want, than try to remove excess paint if you use too much.

- Carefully remove the stencil while the paint is wet (this prevents the dry paint from 'gluing' the stencil to the wood and spoiling the finish when you try to remove it) and leave to dry.

DIE-CUT STENCILS

You can buy these from your local craft store or online. Alternatively, if you have a die-cutting machine designed for scrapbooking, you can use it to create your own stencil.

PERFECT RESULTS

To achieve professional-looking results, hold the brush perpendicular to the wood and carefully dab the paint onto the stencil to fill in the letters, making sure it covers the edges so that each letter is filled in.

Garden Planter

Show off your green fingers and your carpentry skills with this easy upcycled planter. Use reclaimed wood in different widths and painted in several colours to ensure there is plenty of visual interest.

MATERIALS

Piece of 2cm (¾in) plywood, 30.5cm (12in) square

Reclaimed painted pieces of wood, 30.5cm (12in) tall. You will need enough pieces to measure about 122cm (48in) wide in total when placed side by side

Four pieces of reclaimed wood, 38cm (15in) long

Four pieces of wood, cut into isosceles triangles and with the equal sides both 6.3cm (2½in) long

32–36 screws, 4mm ($^3\!/_{16}$in) in diameter and 4cm (1⅝in) long

TOOLS

Table saw

Mitre saw

Drill with drill bit the same size as the screws and drill bit desired size for drainage holes

Screwdriver bit

Measuring tape

Pencil

Garden Planter

1 Place the plywood square on a flat surface. Join the pieces of reclaimed wood to the edges of the square and at right-angles to it to create the sides of the planter. To do this, drill pilot holes through each side piece and into the base. Secure with screws. Repeat until all the pieces of reclaimed wood are secured around the base.

2 To secure the top corner at each side, drill a pilot hole through the section where the sides join 2.5cm (1in) from top and then secure with a screw.

3 To make the top of the sides, mitre the ends of the 38cm (15in) long pieces of reclaimed wood. Turn the mitre saw to a 45-degree angle and cut both ends of each piece of wood so that the shorter, inside edge of the mitred wood measures 30.5cm (12in) long.

4 Arrange the pieces of mitred wood on the top of the sides of the planter, so that the inside edge is flush with the side piece and the ridge hangs slightly over the outside of the planter. Drill two pilot holes and then secure with screws.

5 Drill three large holes into the base for drainage.

6 With the bottom of the planter facing up, secure a wood triangle at each corner to act as feet. Drill pilot holes and then secure with screws.

Bath Tray

This handy tray will hold everything you need for a relaxing soak in the tub and it takes less than 60 minutes to make! Because it will get wet, use a mould- and mildew-resistant waterproof sealant.

MATERIALS

Four pieces of reclaimed wood, 76cm (30in) long

Two pieces of reclaimed wood, 35.5cm (14in) long

Polyurethane waterproof sealant

Eight 2cm (¾in) screws

TOOLS

Sandpaper

Brush

Carpenter's square (square ruler)

Clamp

Drill with drill bit the same size as the screws

Piece of scrap cardboard

Paintbrush to apply sealant

Bath Tray

1 Sand the edges of each piece of wood, then brush off any excess dust or debris.

2 Assemble the tray upside down. Place the four long planks side by side and use the carpenter's square to make sure the edges are correctly aligned.

3 Use the clamp to secure the planks together so they are tightly held in place. Use the carpenter's square to make sure each corner forms a right angle.

4 Position the two shorter pieces of wood on each side of the tray, running across the long planks. Remember to place them so that they will sit inside your bath widthways. Drill very shallow pilot holes in the two short pieces of wood – they should only be deep enough to break through the first layer of wood.

5 Drill all the screws into the pilot holes, being careful to ensure all four pieces are held together tightly and the bottom small pieces are flush with the top tray pieces.

6 Brush off the excess dust and debris from all the surfaces of the tray. Protecting the work surface with scrap cardboard, paint the wood with sealant. Start on the underside, focusing on the edges, ends and gaps between the pieces of wood. Leave to dry completely before flipping over and painting the top of the tray.

TIP
Be sure to use screws that are long enough to connect the two pieces of wood but do not breach the top of the tray.

Easy Pallet Shelving

This project is a great example of creative upcycling! Turn a pallet into a beautiful rustic statement piece that is the perfect place to store a favourite book or display treasured keepsakes. You only need a section of the pallet – or more of it to make a set of matching shelves.

MATERIALS

Pallet

Six screws, 4mm (³⁄₁₆in) in diameter and 4cm (1⅝in) long

Wood stain

Hanger that will hold the weight of the shelf

TOOLS

Ruler

Pencil

Circular saw

Hammer

Drill with drill bit to fit existing holes in the wood

Screwdriver bit

Hand sander with 60 or 80 grit sandpaper

Scrap cardboard or newspaper

Latex gloves

Rag

Scrap cardboard or newspaper

Easy Pallet Shelving

1 The shelf consists of a 35.5cm (14in) deep section of the pallet with two pieces of the top deck board and the supports, plus an additional plank that serves as the backing. To separate the main section from the pallet, use a ruler and pencil to measure and mark a line on each runner 35.5cm (14in) from one long edge of the pallet. Use a circular saw to cut along the lines on each side of the pallet.

2 To cut through the middle section of the pallet, lay the pallet down on the ground and cut from the top to remove the 35.5cm (14in) deep section of the pallet.

3 Remove one board from the remaining pallet by hammering the back (reverse end) of the nails to loosen them. Then use the claw of the hammer to take off the board. Discard the nails and the rest of the pallet.

4 Place the 35.5cm (14in) section of pallet on the ground so that the top deck board timbers are on the bottom. Place the single board across the section of pallet to create the shelf backing. Secure in place by inserting screws through the holes left by the nails.

5 Use the hand sander to sand all the surfaces of the wood to smooth them and remove any splinters but be careful to keep the rustic appearance.

6 Using scrap cardboard or newspaper to protect the work surface and gloves to protect your hands, use a rag to apply a generous amount of wood stain to the shelf. Leave to dry.

7 Attach the hanger to the back of the frame. Drill pilot holes into the frame and then secure the hanger with screws.

TIP

Look for a hanger designed for paintings or heavy photo frames with a 11kg (25lb) rating. You can use a single hanger in the centre of the shelf, or put one on each side of the back to make it even more secure. This is essential if you plan to put heavy items on the shelf.

Timber Timepiece

As well as always knowing the time, you will have a sense of accomplishment every time you look up at this clock. The reclaimed wood face conceals a battery-operated clock mechanism; similar kits are available from craft stores or online – choose one that suits your decor.

MATERIALS

Five pieces of reclaimed wood, 36.6cm (14½in) long, about 7.6cm (3in) wide

Two pieces of wood, 30.5cm (12in) long, 1.3cm (½in) thick

Clock kit

Ten 2cm (¾in) screws

TOOLS

Drill

Drill bit the same size as screws

Drill bit the same size as clock hardware

33cm (13in) diameter plate or similar item to use as a template

Pencil

Jigsaw

Hand sander

Timber Timepiece

1 Place the five pieces of reclaimed wood on a flat surface so that they are aligned and face down. Place one of the support pieces at each end of the reclaimed wood slats so that they are at right angles to them and about 7.6cm (3in) from the ends. Drill five pilot holes into each support piece to join each piece of reclaimed wood to both supports. Be sure not to drill through to the clock face. Insert the screws to secure the clock face to the supports.

2 Turn the joined wood over. Using a pencil and a large plate or similar item as a template, draw a 33cm (13in) diameter circle onto the wood for the clock face. Cut along the marked line using the jigsaw.

3 Use a hand sander to smooth the cut edges of the wood.

4 Find the centre of the clock face by measuring it vertically and horizontally and marking the point where the lines intersect. Drill a hole the same size as the clock kit hardware at the centre point.

5 Insert the clock mechanism through the hole and screw it in place until it is snug. Following the package instructions, attach the clock kit base washer, small locking nut, hour hand, minute hand, locking nut and second hand.

TIP

The two pieces of wood measuring 30.6cm (12in) long are used to support the clock face. They must be thick enough to hold the clock kit and allow the finished clock to sit flush against the wall. For the kit used here, the wood was 1.3cm (½in) thick, but check your kit before choosing your wood.

Techniques

Some of the techniques used for working with found wood are the same as for any other type of wood. This section tells you what tools you will need and how to use them, as well as showing you how to tie some handy knots. The real joy of working with found wood is in the finding. We tell you where to look and what to look out for!

Choosing and Using Found Wood

Driftwood

Bleached and beautiful, smoothed and silky, driftwood is one of my favourite materials. It lives up to its name, having spent time in the water drifting, floating and being tumbled by river currents or ocean waves, and sometimes both! The wood may be deposited on a riverbank or beach to bleach and dry out, only to be picked up and carried on another journey by high tides or river flows. If only the wood could tell us about its journey! Driftwood may originate from high in the mountain forests, it might have been part of a boat that was lost at sea (be aware that it is technically illegal to take salvage), or it could be an ocean pier that succumbed to the power of the currents. Coming in all shapes and sizes, driftwood looks great when it has been tossed by the water and aged and bleached by the sun. Its naturally rounded edges and soft grey-white colours give it an ageless appeal.

Choosing and Using Found Wood

WHERE TO LOOK

Since the wood is shaped by water through the tumbling action of surf or the swirl of a swiftly moving current, beaches are the best places to find driftwood. But not just any beach or shore will yield treasure. The best places to find driftwood, providing you have the permission of the landowner, are within a mile or two of the mouth of a river or on a beach that has strong currents. You are less likely to find it in a tranquil bay.

Look for a naturally flowing river that has not been dammed and that has a year-round rather than a seasonal flow. Wood carried by wild and natural rivers comes from fallen trees and branches.

Avoid rivers that are surrounded by housing developments or urban sprawl, as they do not yield much driftwood. When people live near rivers, they tend to want to control and tame the water for their own benefit, so losing the natural strength of the water that washes wood downstream.

The beaches of northern California, Oregon and Washington state are my happy hunting ground. They are incredible places to find driftwood, from small pieces that fit in your pocket to giant tree trunks and huge branches that can take two or more people to carry. They are brought to the Pacific Ocean by fast-flowing rivers with thick forests growing right to the water's edge. The ocean currents are very strong and many beaches are littered with naturally aged and tumbled driftwood. Even if you do not live near the sea, you should be able to find a river or lake that will reward you with great driftwood finds.

WHAT TO LOOK FOR

When choosing driftwood, it really comes down to what you like and what is available. If there is an abundance of wood, you can afford to be more selective. At other times, make do with what you find. We love wood that has been naturally worn and 'sanded' by the elements and bleached by the sun. If there is a lot of wood on a beach, look above the high-tide line. This is where you will find the wood that has been on the beach longest, perhaps deposited by a storm surge or a super-high tide and left to bleach and age. Take your time: the search for the right piece of driftwood is as much fun as the joy when you find it.

PREPARING THE DRIFTWOOD

I do not do much to the wood besides thoroughly drying it and then brushing any loose sand or debris off the surface with a soft brush. However, some people soak the wood in fresh water to remove any salt water. Be careful not to brush or clean too much because you risk losing the patina that nature provided, and you may scratch the wood if it is soft or wet.

For small pieces of driftwood, soaking in bleach and water lightens the wood and kills any critters. Make a soaking mixture using 500ml (17½fl oz) of bleach to 4.5l (8 pints) of water. Put your driftwood pieces in a bucket and add enough of the mixture to cover. If the pieces float, use a flat rock to keep them submerged. Leave for five days, changing the bleach water daily. Drain and allow them to dry naturally.

Logs

If you have the landowner's permission, look for logs in hard-to-reach places, perhaps where they have been embedded between large rocks or boulders on a riverbank edge or on the edge of a forest. You can also buy logs (see page 126). Bought logs will have been heat-treated and so have the advantage of being bug free. If you know anyone who has had to cut down a tree, ask them for a log or two.

Use hardwood such as ash, birch, beech, cherry, elm, maple or oak rather than softwood such as pine or spruce.
The log should feel heavy. Choose solid pieces that are free from decay. To check that the wood is suitable, bang it against a rock – if there is a dull thud, it is rotten. Do not bother with it!

Use a soft brush to clean off dirt and debris, then spray with insecticide (see below). If there is any rot, cut around it.

COMMON HARDWOOD TREES IN THE UK

- ash: genus *Fraxinus*
- beech: genus *Fagus*
- birch: genus *Betula*
- cedar: genus *Cedrus*
- cherry: genus *Prunus*
- elm: genus *Ulmus*
- holly: genus *Ilex*
- larch: genus *Larix*
- maple: genus *Acer*
- oak: genus *Quercus*
- poplar: genus *Populus*
- red alder: genus *Alnus*
- sycamore: genus *Platanus*
- walnut: genus *Juglans*
- willow: genus *Salix*
- yew: genus *Taxus*

MAKE IT PEST FREE

Found wood might have been someone else's home before you moved it into your own! To avoid bringing any creepy-crawlies inside, you will need to treat the wood with an insecticide. Mix insecticide with water in a spray bottle. Take the wood you are treating outside and place it on newspaper or cardboard to avoid getting the insecticide on any surfaces. Spray each piece thoroughly with the insecticide mixture. Leave to dry naturally – large pieces may take a few days to dry completely.

Twigs and Branches

You can find fallen twigs and branches in your own garden or in public woodlands. Be sure to take only fallen twigs or branches; do not cut them from living trees (unless they belong to you, of course). Be careful to avoid trespassing on private property and check regulations relating to taking wood in public woodlands (see page 113).

Look for interesting shapes or colours. I always keep an eye out for branches from less common trees and for gnarled roots with character. Pick up wood that is the right size for the project you are planning. Even small twigs can be used, as in the Twig Vase (see page 10), while a group of branches can add interest to your hallway as a Rustic Coat Rack (see page 32).

I find that Mother Nature has usually taken care of most of the cleaning, so just spot clean with a brush as necessary. However, if your finds are muddy or dirty, you will need to rinse them in water and scrub with a wire brush. If the mud is dry, let the wood soak until any dirt is soft enough to come off easily. You do not want to scrub so hard that you remove the bark. Allow the wood to dry naturally in a well-ventilated room.

Boards

Old boards can be found almost everywhere; you might even have some in your garage. When you are out looking for driftwood, you may come across sea-weathered boards. You can also break up old pallets and crates; look for them at car boot fairs.

If you want a weathered look, seek out wood that has been exposed to the elements, such as driftwood, weathered crates or pallets, collapsed barns or sheds or old doors.

Be sure not to trespass and do not take anything without asking the property owner for permission.

Old boards may have nails. Remove these first. Then use a brush to clean off dirt and debris. Boards have often been painted. I love the look of weathered paint and only remove loose or flaking paint. Be sure to wear a mask and dispose of the flakes appropriately, as the paint may contain lead.

As with all found wood, insects may be present, so the wood will need to be treated (see page 111) before you bring it indoors.

STAY LEGAL

Unless you are on your own property or on that of someone who has given you permission to gather wood, you will need to obey local or national laws. Countries, and even counties, have different rules. In California, for example, the official limit for taking driftwood is 50 lbs (23kg) per person, per day, as long as the wood is taken from above the high-tide line. In contrast, on the Shetland Islands, in Scotland, driftwood on the strand line belongs to the person who finds it; if it has been drawn up to the upper shore, it belongs to the person who put it there. Broadly speaking, in the UK, land above the high water mark is usually owned by an individual or the local authority; land below this point is most likely owned by the Crown Estate. Obtain permission from the owner before taking anything.

GATHERING DRIFTWOOD

Be sure to check the wood for living organisms, such as crabs, which may be using it as a home. Look out, too, for nesting birds. If you do not live near a suitable beach or riverbank, you can also buy driftwood online (see page 126).

GATHERING WOOD

You are unlikely to get into trouble for picking up the few fallen twigs needed to make the Twig Vase (see page 10), but taking large logs and branches may be another matter and permission should be sought from the landowner. In the UK, estover rights (the right to take wood on common land) enshrined in the Magna Carta came to an end in 2008. However, a few places still allow small-scale foraging for wood. An old by-law in Epping Forest in Essex, for example, allows visitors to take up to 12kg (26lbs) of wood. The Forestry Commission, which owns many woodlands, supplies permits for dead-wood removal in some areas, particularly in northern and central England. Such arrangements are at the discretion of the local office.

DO NOT SPREAD DISEASE

In recent years, the risk of spreading infestations of insects by moving firewood long distances has become better known. When gathering wood for your projects, it is best to find it within 16km (10 miles) of where you live. Wood that has been kiln dried at a temperature of 70°C (160°F) for at least 75 minutes is safe. If buying online, be sure that you are buying kiln-dried wood.

Tools and Equipment

THE ESSENTIALS
- Sandpaper (100–180 grit), glue, screws and/or nails, screwdrivers (Phillips-head and flat-head), carpenter's square, hammer, handsaw, wood file, paintbrushes, clamps.

ADVANCED ITEMS
- Power drill, mitre saw, table saw, palm sander, planer, circular saw.

SAFETY EQUPMENT
- Plastic/rubber gloves.
- Goggles or protective eyeglasses.
- Dust mask.

HOW TO CARE FOR YOUR TOOLS
- Store indoors away from the elements, clean on a regular basis, lubricate moving parts following the manufacturer's instructions, change blades as needed.

HAND TOOLS VS. POWER TOOLS
- Hand tools can be essential when adding finishing touches to a piece. Sanding by hand, adding a screw in a small space, or adding a protective finish are often things that can only be done by hand. Power tools, however, are essential for cutting wood to save time and energy.

SAFETY

Always wear a mask and eye protection while working with wood, paints, stains and other finishes, and be sure to follow any safety advice on labels. Do not use power tools without proper training.

HAND PLANERS

A planer is great for levelling surfaces. The Trio of Coat Hooks (see page 24) uses the planer to give a flat surface for mounting on the wall. However, a planer is not a tool that you will use on every project, so it is a luxury rather than a must-have. When using a planer, be sure to place both hands in the correct position for equal pressure. Do not press down hard on the surface being levelled – let the tool do the work. Start on one end of the surface to be planed and move slowly and methodically to the other end. Be consistent in moving in one direction. As with sanding, go 'with the grain', following the direction of the long grain.

TOOL	WHAT IS IT USED FOR?	WHY IS IT WORTH HAVING IN YOUR TOOL BOX?
Table saw	straight cuts on large wood	essential for big cuts
Mitre saw	angle and end cuts	for angle cuts
Circular saw	fast straight-line cutting	versatile and mobile
Planer	levelling uneven surfaces	for a professional finish
Drill with drill bits	making solid joints and connecting pieces of wood with screws and bolts	to save time and effort
Palm sander	finishing work, levelling work	for a professional finish
Tape measure	measuring	for accuracy
Phillips-head screwdriver	screwing in Phillips-head screws	Phillips-head screws are the most common type
Scissors	cutting rope	essential
Paintbrushes	applying finishes	essential
Clamps	holding pieces of wood together while wood glue is setting	for secure bonds

Measuring and Sawing

MEASURING TECHNIQUES

As the old saying goes, measure twice, cut once! In other words, avoid errors by checking your measurements two or three times before cutting your materials. When measuring for a cut, remember that the cut should be made on the outside of the measurement (on the side you will not be using). If you cut right on the line, the blade of the saw will reduce the measurement, making it shorter than you require.

A thumb lock on the front of the tape measure allows you to lock the tape measure to a certain length. Always mark your measurements in pencil so that you can erase any stray marks once a job is complete.

A speed carpenter's square is a great tool. Use it to measure corners and right angles quickly and accurately. It typically has a lipped edge that can be pressed against the flat side of a piece of wood to ensure greater accuracy.

SAWING TECHNIQUES

Always wear protective eyewear when using power tools. You do not want anything getting caught in the machinery, so do not wear loose scarves, jewellery, gloves or belts.

When using a handsaw, make sure your support hand is clear of the cutting line and the movement of the blade. And go slowly, keeping the blade on the line. The cutting action is the downwards stroke, when you put pressure on the saw and the wood. The upwards stroke brings the saw back into the cutting position.

When using a table saw or circular saw, remember that the blade is moving at high speed and can catch and cause injury if you try to force it through the wood. Be patient and let the saw blade do its job. Forcing a circular saw through hardwood or forcing hardwood through a table saw can cause inaccurate cuts and possible injury.

Knots

TYING A SIMPLE KNOT

For simple projects, sometimes all it takes is a simple knot! To tie such a knot, make a loop and insert one end of the string into the loop, then pull both ends in opposite directions.

MAKING A DOUBLE KNOT

Sometimes a sturdier knot is called for, and in that case you may want to use a double knot – like the simple knot, but with another loop! To tie a double knot, make a loop and insert one end of the string into the loop (steps 1 and 2). Before pulling both ends taut, insert the same end of the string into the loop again (3). Now gently pull both ends of the string taut (4) to create the double knot (5).

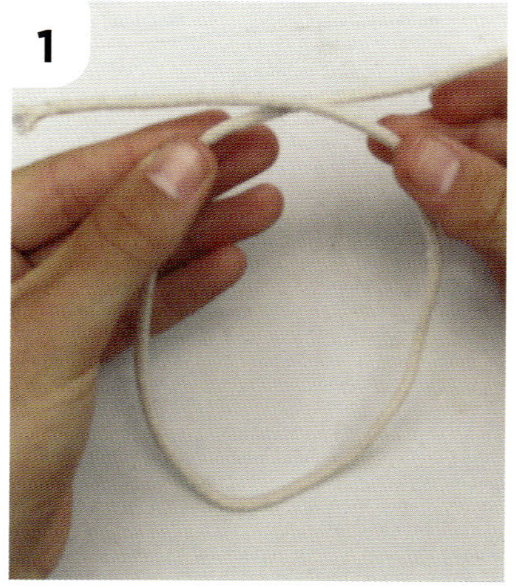

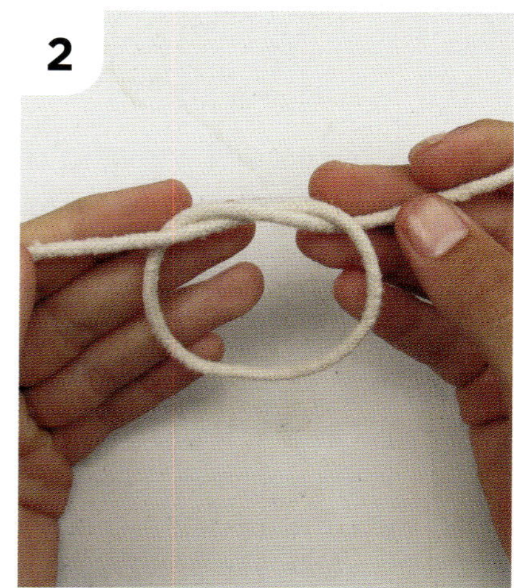

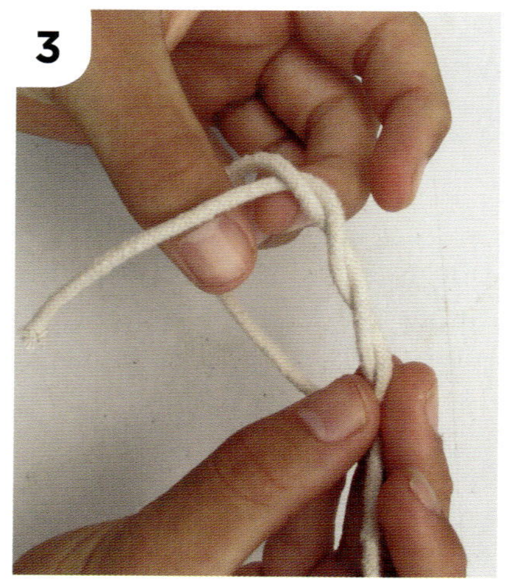

TYING AN UNDER-WRITER'S KNOT

For projects involving electrical wiring, an underwriter's knot is best. To make such a knot, first separate the two wires. (We have used string to show how to tie this knot.) Place the two wires parallel to each other (1). Form a loop with the first wire so that the bent end passes behind the cord (2), then make a loop with the other wire so that the bent end passes in front of the cord (3). You should now have two loops, one with the end passing around the back and one passing in front. Feed the loose end of each wire through the loop of the opposite wire (4) and pull the two ends in opposite directions (5)!

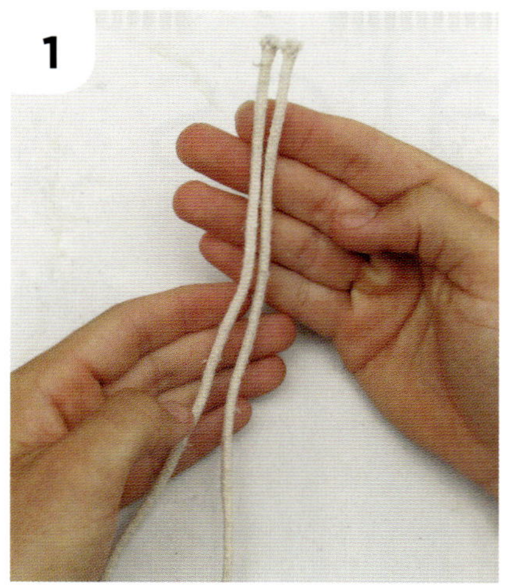

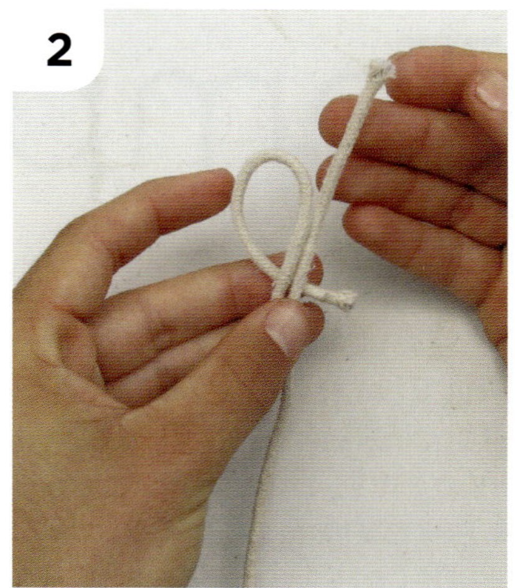

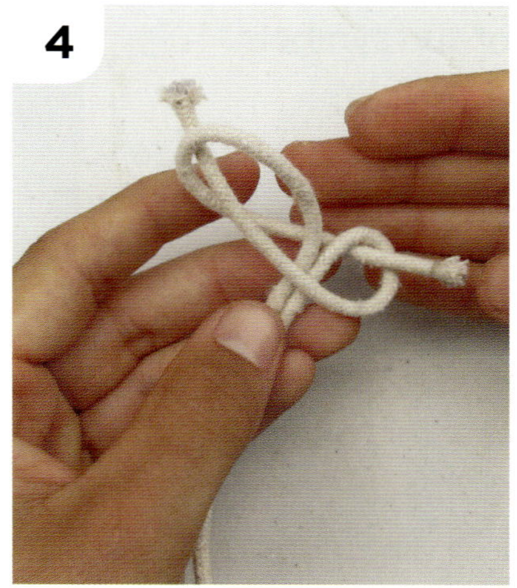

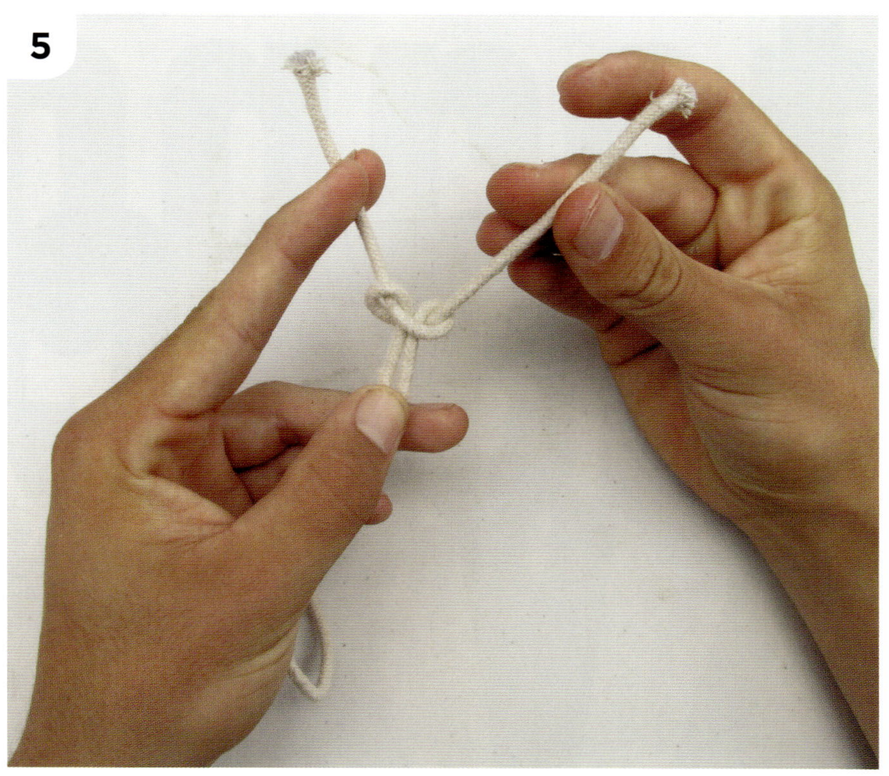

Resources

PAINT AND BRUSHES

Hobbycraft: www.hobbycraft.co.uk
Rymans: www.rymans.co.uk
The Works: www.theworks.co.uk

WOOD AND TOOLS

Woodworkers Workshop: www.woodworkersworkshop.co.uk
Yandles: www.yandles.co.uk

LOGS, BRANCHES, AND DRIFTWOOD

Etsy: www.etsy.com

HARDWARE AND MISCELLANEOUS SUPPLIES

eBay: www.ebay.co.uk
Amazon: www.amazon.co.uk

SHELLS

Dorset Gifts: www.dorsetgifts.com
Online Shells: www.onlineshells.co.uk

Index

Acknowledgements

Linda Suster would like to thank:
Mike Suster, Megan Suster, Jack Suster, Emma Suster,
Abby Suster, Calvin Suster and Steve Moreno-Terrill.

Toucan Books would like to thank:
Penelope Armitage, Charlotte Cox, Dave Ham,
and Antonia and Peter van der Meer.